D1798842

LifeLine

BIBLE STUDY GUIDES

♦ For Small Group or Personal Study ♦

BOOK TWO

Kurt Johnson

North American Church Resources
and
Review and Herald® Publishing Association
Hagerstown, Maryland

North American Church Resources provides materials for local churches in the United States, Canada, and Bermuda

Editing and page composition by Ken McFarland, Rae Patterson
Charts by Lant Colburn, used by permission of Seminars Unlimited
Cover design by Helcio Deslandes

Unless otherwise noted, all Bible texts are from The New King James Version. Copyright © 1979, 1980, 1982, Thomas Nelson, Inc., Publishers.

ISBN: 0-8280-0975-9

LIFELINE BIBLE STUDY GUIDES

Title	Topic
Book 1	
1. The Bible—Can I trust It?	Origin and Use of the Bible
2. God—Who Is He?	Father, Son, Holy Spirit
3. Created With You in Mind!	Creation of Earth
4. Created for a Purpose	God's Plan for Man
5. Freedom in Jeopardy	How Sin Began
6. Jesus—His Identity	Understanding Jesus
7. Set Free!	Plan of Salvation
8. A Symbol of Freedom	Baptism
9. Called For a Purpose	God's Church
10. Guidelines for Daily Living	Ten Commandments
11. Obedience By Choice	Law and Grace
12. A Day With the Son	Sabbath—Part 1
13. God's Sabbath—Its Meaning	Sabbath—Part 2
Book 2	
14. Signposts	Signs of Christ's Coming
15. How Will Jesus Return?	Second Coming
16. Death—Then What?	Understanding Death
17. Sin—Forever Gone	Millennium/Hell
18. Forever Young	Heaven/New Earth
19. Symbols of Salvation	Old Testament Sanctuary
20. The Future Predicted	End-time Prophecy
21. Symbols of Commitment	Stewardship of Life
22. Life At Its Best	Health/Lifestyle Issues
23. A Family Forever	Christian Fellowship
24. A Messenger for Today	Gift of Prophecy
25. A Spirit-Filled Life	Holy Spirit/Spiritual Gifts
26. Summarizing God's Message	Summary

Contents

Getting Started

These study guides are designed to be used in several ways. You can study them alone, two people can study together, or they can be used in a small group setting involving three or more people.

As you know from studying Book 1 of this series, small group Bible study can be both enjoyable and educational. The goal is for a group of interested people to meet in a home, public meeting room, church, or other location and study God's Word together. Ideally, the group will be made up of three to twelve individuals sitting around a table or in a circle for an hour and a half to two hours, one day a week, studying, praying, and sharing together.

Prayer, Bible information, and opinions will be part of the group discussion. All discussion and prayer should be voluntary. As a general rule, do not go around the circle for prayer, answers, or discussion. Allow for spontaneous, voluntary responses.

Three things are essential to all group Bible studies. Those essentials are—

- ■ Sharing (getting better acquainted with one another)
- ■ Bible study (understanding and learning about God's Word)
- ■ Prayer (applying what we learn and asking God to assist us.)

The format in these study guides is based on these three essentials and will be similar in each study. The topics in the series are listed on page 3.

May God guide you as you study, is my prayer!
—*Kurt Johnson*

14

Signposts

GROUP LIFE

Growing Together—Effective Group Communication

Communication is the key to good relationships. People who have participated in groups identify five levels of communication that impact the growth of the member and group. These areas are:

■ **Cliché Conversation:** This is the "testing the waters" stage. The group members' responses are largely surface remarks that are non-committal or nonthreatening.

■ **Reporting Facts:** The member simply gives surface responses to the discussion without personal application to daily life.

■ **Ideas and Judgments:** At this level, the member begins to share ideas, observing how the others react. If the ideas receive a positive response, the member ventures to the next level.

■ **Feelings and Emotions.** At this juncture, the group member talks openly about how the scripture impacts his or her current situation and daily life.

■ **Openness and Personal Commitment:** At this level, a person feels assured that he or she is accepted by the group no matter what they say or how they react.

Sharing Life

As your group meets each week, various needs are shared. These needs reflect the needs we observe in the world around us. From your perspective, what is one of the greatest needs in the world today?

SCRIPTURE AND LIFE

WHAT JESUS SAID ABOUT HIS SECOND COMING

". . . I go to prepare a place for you. And if I go and prepare a place for you, I will come again and receive you to Myself; that where I am, there you may be also."—John 14:2, 3

As you study, be thinking about the LifeQuest questions:
- ■ What does this topic tell me about God?
- ■ What difference does this topic make in my daily life?
- ■ How does this topic help me in my relationship with Jesus?

The author of the book of Hebrews says: "So Christ was offered once to bear the sins of many. To those who eagerly wait for Him, He will appear a second time, apart from sin for salvation." Heb. 9:28. In this New Testament passage, the return of Christ is qualified by the adjective "second." Jesus promised He would come again (John 14:3); the angels said He would come as He left (Acts 1:11). The hope of Christianity is that someday Jesus will return to this earth.

❑ Both the Old and New Testaments predict the second coming of Jesus. Read the following Scripture passages and discuss their messages: Psalm 50:3-5; John 14:1-3. When you think about Christ's coming, how do you feel?

___excited	___mixed emotions
___afraid	___other _____
___ready	

If you are afraid, what makes you feel the way you do?_____

When will Jesus return? His return has been predicted at various times; however, He still has not returned. No one on earth—not even the angels in heaven—has been given that information. (Matthew 24:36.) One might not know the day or hour, but Jesus and the New Testament writers talked about how to know when Jesus' return is near.

One day, as Jesus was leaving the temple in Jerusalem, He told the disciples that someday the temple would be destroyed. The amazed disciples later asked Jesus, as He sat upon the Mount of Olives, to tell them about this event and about the end of the world.

❑   Read the discussion in Matthew. 24:1-3.

◆   Review verses 4-31 and list the points you discover under the following headings:

Signs in the Natural World_____

_____

Signs in the Political World_____

_____

Signs in the Religious World_____

_____

◆   Reflect on and discuss the following points.

✔   How can you distinguish a false Christ and a false prophet from the genuine?_____

_____

✔   List any places around the world you can think of where currently war, famine, earthquakes, suffering, or pestilences (scourges) are occurring:

_____

❑   Matthew does not mention the signs in the social world preceding Jesus' coming. However, to understand the complete picture, read the following texts and write down the signs you discover. 2 Timothy 3:1-5; Romans 1:28-32_____

_____

❑ Read Matthew 24:36-51. How does this passage make you feel?

___The world today is like it was in Noah's time.
___I don't like to think about this topic.
___I want Jesus to wait a while before He comes.
___Other _____

How would you change your life to prepare for Christ's coming?

_____

❑ Matthew 24 and its parallel chapter (Luke 21) mention several events that have been fulfilled and documented. This section will refer to these events and give sources for further study.

1. The destruction of Jerusalem in A.D. 70 (Matthew 24:15-20; Luke 21:20-24). Historians tell us that the city of Jerusalem was surrounded by Roman troops under the leadership of Cestius Gallus in November of A.D. 66. The soldiers suddenly withdrew, which provided an opportunity for the Christians in Jerusalem to flee. The Roman troops returned in A.D. 70 and captured the city. *(God Cares,* vol. II, p. 25, Maxwell.)

2. In comparing the following scriptures with events of the past, many Bible students are convinced that these prophecies have already been fulfilled. The suggested events are well worth investigating. Matthew 24:29 says, "The sun will be darkened," "the moon will not give its light," and "the stars will fall from heaven." Revelation 6:12, 13 tells of a "great earthquake," adding that the "moon became like blood," and that the "stars of the sky fell to the earth."

■ The Lisbon Earthquake. Nov. 1, 1755.

This earthquake is listed in almanacs and encyclopedias as one of the major earthquakes of world history. The quake caused tidal waves and disturbances some 4,000 miles away. It also drew many people to consider their relationship with God. *(God Cares,* vol. II, pp. 195, 196, Maxwell.)

■ The Sun Darkened. May 19, 1780.

A 25,000-mile area in the eastern United States was darkened so that it appeared as night during the daytime. The event significantly impacted the religious thinking of many people. (*God Cares,* vol. II, p.196, Maxwell.)

■ Star Shower. Nov. 13, 1833.

This event took place across vast areas of the United States when stars fell at a rate of 60,000 or more per hour. Many called it a snowstorm of stars. The event caused many to reflect upon prophecies predicting such an episode. (*God Cares,* vol. II, p. 198, Maxwell.)

How well do these events qualify as the fulfillment of Christ's predictions? Each event was notable in its own right. All three events have not been equalled in their magnitude since their occurrence. Jesus said the signs would immediately follow the tribulation of those days, and they did. The evidence reveals that these signs were fulfilled as they followed the described biblical sequence. It is also possible that similar events may occur again at Jesus' second coming.

As it tells of Christ's coming, the Bible describes nature being shaken out of its normal course (Revelation 6:14-17; Revelation 16:17-21).

(Ask your group leader about study guides or booklets that will help you to understand the prophecies explaining end-time events.)

❏ LIFEQUEST—Thoughtfully review these questions:
  ■ What does this topic tell me about God?
  ■ What difference does this topic make in my daily life?
  ■ How does this topic help me in my relationship with Jesus?

APPLICATION TO LIFE

Real Life

Joe attended almost every evangelistic series of meetings or religious seminar that came to town. He also attended church quite consistently. However, Joe never seemed to make a commitment to God or to anything related to religion.

The pastor of the church Joe attended decided to visit him and discuss this with him. However, when the pastor asked Joe why he had never made a commitment to Jesus Christ, Joe attempted to change the subject. The pastor kindly persisted. Eventually Joe responded.

Joe replied by telling the pastor that he attended the meetings and church services to make sure he understood Scripture. He said he knew the steps he needed to take to accept Jesus into his life but that he was not ready. There were some things in his life that he did not want to give up. He said he had studied the signs of the end of the world and had decided that when the signs were about to be fulfilled—or when he knew he was nearing the end of his life—then he would be willing to accept Jesus completely as his Lord and Saviour.

Your Turn

The signs of Jesus' coming are not to be used as a gauge as to when to accept Jesus. Matthew 24:44 says, "Be ready, for the Son of Man is coming at an hour you do not expect Him." The signs are an assurance of the reality of Jesus' coming.

Check the statements that most closely reflect your current feelings. (These are for personal reflection, not group discussion.)

___ I am thankful for the signs that point toward Jesus' second coming. I am looking forward to His coming and plan to be ready for it.

___ I have some unanswered questions concerning the signs and want to spend more time discussing the topic.

___ I believe I have a good understanding of the topic, but I'm still thinking about how I will respond in my life. Continue to pray for me.

___ Other_____

Alone With God

Some Christians make the mistake of worrying about whether every event of daily life—or every major news story—has significance as a sign of the end. This can be very stressful. The best way to prepare for Christ's coming is to recommit your life to God each day and to spend daily time with Him. If your heart is right, you will be ready no matter what occurs.

15

How Will
Jesus Return?

GROUP LIFE

Growing Together—Competition and Group Life

In order for a Bible study group to be a positive experience, a group member must be interested in not only sharing information, but in listening to others. When members begin to act as if they have all the answers and no one else has any new thoughts, the group is stifled. In fact, a sure way to destroy a group and make it a less-than-enjoyable experience is for members to develop the attitude that they must always be out to win!

Several steps can assist in keeping a group from suffering because of competition in providing answers and in group participation.

These steps include:

(1) Showing empathy and respect for the person speaking.

(2) Encouraging each group member to express his or her opinion.

(3) Modeling love, acceptance, and listening as part of one's lifestyle.

Sharing Life

Most people have a place in the United States they would like to visit someday. If you had the chance, where would you like to visit, and why?

SCRIPTURE AND LIFE

WHAT JESUS SAID ABOUT HIS SECOND COMING

"For the Son of Man will come in the glory of His Father with His angels, and then He will reward each according to his works."—Matthew 16:27

As you study, be thinking about the LifeQuest questions:

■ What does this topic tell me about God?

■ What difference does this topic make in my daily life?

■ How does this topic help me in my relationship with Jesus?

In the study guide discussing the signs of Christ's coming, Matthew 24:37-39 is cited. It reads: "But as the days of Noah were, so also will the coming of the Son of Man be. For as in the days before the flood, they were eating and drinking, marrying and giving in marriage, until the day that Noah entered the ark, and did not know until the flood came and took them all away, so also will the coming of the Son of Man be."

This scripture says that as people are going about the routine of daily living, Jesus will burst upon the scene and end life here as we know it. For some, the thought of Jesus' coming strikes fear and apprehension in their heart. For others, it brings excitement and joy.

❑ The Scriptures give information concerning the certainty that Jesus will return. Read John 14:1-4 and then check and discuss your response.

____Jesus said not to be troubled, but I am troubled about His coming.

____I know the "way" that Jesus is referring to in verse 4.

____I am hiding from God.

____I am momentarily taking a side trip in my life.

____I have already asked Jesus to reserve space for me!

◆ Read 2 Peter 3:1-13. How do Creation and the Flood

support the fact that Jesus will return and the earth be destroyed (verses 3-7)?_____

_____

In your opinion, what determines the length of God's patience or waiting?_____

Discuss the key points or questions you may have concerning 2 Peter 3._____

❑ Read the following texts, then discuss and list what information you discover in regard to the seven listed categories. Matthew 16:27; Matthew 24:23-31; Acts 1:9-11; 1 Thessalonians 4:16; 5:1-11; Revelation 1:7; Revelation 6:12-17; Revelation 16:17-21.

◆ audible return _____
◆ visible return _____
◆ a sudden return _____
◆ a glorious return _____
◆ a personal return _____
◆ effects on the earth _____
◆ other _____

❑ What excites you the most about the second coming of Jesus ?

___seeing Jesus in person   ___living forever with Jesus,
___listening to the angels sing   friends and family
___knowing that sin will end   ___other_____

❑ LIFEQUEST—Thoughtfully review these questions:
 ■ What does this topic tell me about God?
 ■ What difference does this topic make in my daily life?
 ■ How does this topic help me in my relationship with Jesus?

APPLICATION TO LIFE

Real Life

Lee was an elderly gentleman living in a retirement home in the southeastern part of Washington State. Even though the grounds upon which the home was located provided adequate room on which to live, Lee always wanted to be going somewhere. Sometimes he would go to a movie, shopping, or to church. He was never content unless he had a small trip in his plans.

One Sunday evening in August, Lee went to church. The topic that evening concerned the events that would occur at the second coming of Jesus. For the first time in his life, Lee heard about the falling of the stars, the mountains erupting, earthquakes, and destruction upon the earth. He was shaken as he considered these events. After arriving home that evening, he went outside. As he looked up into the evening sky, he saw a star fall. Terror filled his mind and heart as he remembering from the evening sermon what he'd heard about the falling stars as a sign of the the second coming. In terror, Lee fled to a nearby onion field, where he sought refuge in a storage shed. In fact, he hid out for several months before he was finally located!

Upon being questioned, Lee said he was terrified because he did not know if he was ready for Jesus to come, and he did not know what to do—so he ran.

Your Turn

Maybe in this study, you've read for the first time what the Bible says about the events connected with the second coming of Jesus. If so, maybe you have fears similar to Lee's. Then again, maybe you get excited when you think of the events surrounding the return of Christ, not because you are focusing on the destruction, but because you will get to see Jesus and know that this world of sin is ending.

Many people find it hard to comprehend all the details which surround the end of the world. It becomes mind boggling as they consider the world being shaken out of order. In fact, it is difficult for the finite mind to grasp. Some have found help by recognizing that sin is terrible and destructive. The only way for sin to end is to remove sin and sinners permanently from the earth.

Others struggle with wondering how will they have the strength to stand faithful to God during earth's closing events. Some also worry about their physical and mental stamina. These same concerns probably plagued the minds of God's people throughout periods of Christian persecution. The way those faithful ones stood firm for God is the same way God's people will stand firm in the future. The formula is short and simple. Do not worry about that over which you have no control. God is the Creator and is in charge. He will take care of His people. Ask Him for the strength of His Spirit each day, and when the events of the end arrive, He who has guided you each day will continue to do so. Trusting in divine strength has always helped Christians survive.

Check the statements that most closely reflect your current feelings. (These are for personal reflection, not group discussion.)

____I thank God for His biblical description of the events of the second coming. I am looking forward to the day and am trusting Christ as my Saviour and strength.

____I love Jesus and desire to see His coming. However, I am apprehensive about the time of the end. Please pray for me that I will be at peace about this topic.

____I am not yet ready to make a response yet concerning my feelings about the second coming of Jesus. I am still thinking about all that I am studying and learning. Please continue to pray for me.

____Other_____

Alone With God

All Christians desire to grow in faith. Faith brings strength. Take a few days of your devotional time and—using a concordance—look up in the Bible the words *strength, faith, trust, fear,* and *afraid.* As you read the verses, copy the ones that are positive promises from God. Memorize one or two that are especially helpful for you.

16

Death—Then What?

GROUP LIFE

Growing Together—Group Evaluation

The goal of your group is for members to enjoy a positive experience with Jesus and one another. The group needs to periodically spend a few minutes evaluating their experience together.

Sometimes group members prefer not to take the time for evaluation. However, evaluation is always taking place, whether planned or not. But when informal evaluation takes place between one or two members between meetings, the group does not profit and grow from discussing the issues.

Several questions to ask to assist with evaluation are: Are we achieving our purpose? Are we learning biblical material? How well have we been working together? Remember that evaluating your group life is not a negative experience. It is simply a tool to help improve the experience.

Sharing Life

I remember as a boy asking my dad how a bird could fly through the air, pull its wings to its side, and stay in the air without hitting the ground? If you could ask God one puzzling question, what would you ask?

SCRIPTURE AND LIFE

WHAT JESUS SAID ABOUT DEATH

"I am the resurrection and the life. He who believes in Me, though he may die, he shall live."—John 11:25

As you study, be thinking about the LifeQuest questions:

■ What does this topic tell me about God?

■ What difference does this topic make in my daily life?

■ How does this topic help me in my relationship with Jesus?

Genesis 2:7 says, "And the Lord God formed man of the dust of the ground, and breathed into his nostrils the breath of life; and man became a living being [soul]." Here we find God's formula for life (Dust + Life = Living Being [Soul]).

God went on to warn Adam and Eve that disobedience would end their eternal life. Eve told the serpent (Satan) that in regard to the fruit of the tree of knowledge of good and evil, God had said, "You shall not eat it, nor shall you touch it, lest you die."

"And the serpent said to the woman, 'You will not surely die.'" Genesis 3:3, 4.

Satan's first lie to man was that disobedience (sin) does not cause death. The biblical record in Genesis 5:5 states that Adam lived 930 years and then died. Obviously God was correct that man would die. But if this had been the end of the story, life would appear almost meaningless—yet there is hope! The Godhead had formed a plan to allow man to live forever after death! Romans 6:23 says, "For the wages of sin is death, but the gift of God is eternal life in Christ Jesus our Lord."

❑   The present question is: What happens to a man when he dies?

◆   Read John 11:1-44. Have members share in reading portions of this long passage. Then discuss the following questions:

What did Jesus call Lazarus' death? What did He mean?

What do you discover here about death and living again?

_____

What do you discover about Jesus' human feelings?

_____

What does this passage teach you about the resurrection that will occur at "the last day"?

_____

❏ Mark and discuss your response. Spiritually, I feel . . .

___in the grave   ___not sure
___alive, but bound in grave clothes   ___other _____
___alive, resurrected, and set free in Jesus

❏ When you comfort a friend who is grieving, what have you found to be most helpful to them?

___be present and say very little   ___hugging/touching
___share Bible promises (Scripture)   ___listening
___bring food or a gift   ___other _____
___encourage the person to talk

❏ Read 1 Thessalonians 4:13-18. This passage amplifies the story of Lazarus. Discuss and list in order the steps described here.

_____

◆   What does equating death with sleep mean to you personally?

_____

◆   Verse 18 says, "Comfort one another with these words." How do verses 13-18 bring comfort to those who grieve?

_____

❏ Various questions arise concerning death. Choose a section or sections to discuss from the following material. Discuss the sections according to the needs of your Bible study group.

■ **Immortality:** The word translated "immortality" in the Scriptures comes from the Greek words *athanasia* ("deathlessness") and *aphtharsia* ("incorruptible"). Compare the following Scriptures, and discuss the mortality of man and God: 1 Timothy 1:17; 6:15, 16, James 4:13-15, Psalm 78:39.

■ **Hope for Mankind:** Read these passages and discuss how and when man receives immortality: Romans 2:5-7, 1 Corinthians 15:22, 51-58, 1 John 5:11-13.

■ **Death As a Sleep:** As previously discovered, death is called a sleep in Scripture. Read the following passages and discuss what they reveal concerning sleep and man's condition at death: Ecclesiastes 9:5, 6, 10, Psalm 115:17; 146:3, 4, John 5:28, 29.

■ **Spirit:**
a. The word translated "spirit" in the Bible comes from the Hebrew word *ruach* and the Greek word *pneuma*, which mean to blow or breathe. The word is also translated as breath, wind, and courage. The following Scriptures are examples; however, various Bible translations will use the different words interchangeably.

Spirit, Breath: Job 17:1   Courage: Joshua 2:11
Spirit of God: 1 Corinthians 2:11, 14   Wind: John 3:8

b. An interesting passage is Ecclesiastes 3:18-21, which compares the death of humans and animals. Read this passage and discuss what information it adds to your understanding of the subject of the "spirit."

■ **Soul:**
a. The word translated "soul" in the Bible comes from the Hebrew word *nephesh* and the Greek word *psuche*. These words are also

translated as life, person, man, mind, and creature, to name a few. The following Scriptures are examples (though Bible translations will vary).

Life or lives: Matthew 2:20   Mind: Acts 14:2
Living being/creature: Genesis 2:7   Soul: Matthew 10:28

b. In the following Scriptures, the words for soul *(nephesh* and *psuche)* refer to the soul as dying: Judges 16:30 (me = *nephesh*); Ezekiel 18:20. The words *nephesh* and *psuche,* as used in Scripture, reveal that the soul does not live apart from the body.

■   **Summary:** "And may your whole spirit, soul, and body be preserved blameless at the coming of our Lord Jesus Christ."—1 Thessalonians 5:23.

❑ LIFEQUEST—Thoughtfully review these questions:
  ■ What does this topic tell me about God?
  ■ What difference does this topic make in my daily life?
  ■ How does this topic help me in my relationship with Jesus?

APPLICATION TO LIFE

Real Life

Jim's grandma passed away at the age of 96. Jim, being a pastor, was asked by his family to conduct the funeral service. He spoke on John 11, which is the account of the death and resurrection of Lazarus. This chapter touches on sickness, the anticipation of impending death, mourning, friends and family, a funeral, and other related issues. The story of Lazarus also includes an additional dimension of resurrection and renewed life.

Following the funeral, one of Jim's great-aunts said, "I have been thinking about the story of Lazarus. If people go straight to heaven when they die, then Lazarus received a bad deal. If he went to heaven at death, then when Jesus resurrected him, he had to leave the beauty of heaven and come back to the earth and die all over again." Jim looked at his aunt and said, "The problem could be that you do not have the correct understanding of what happens to someone when they die." After a brief discussion, the aunt decided that maybe she should spend more time studying the subject.

Your Turn

There are many viewpoints on the subject of life after death. Within your group, there are probably various views. If after completing this study you find yourself with a different understanding of life after death than before, do not feel bad. The comfort of this topic is knowing that the dead get to sleep in Jesus until the second coming. They have no more suffering, problems, or knowledge of events. The next thing they will know after death is that Jesus is calling them to life to be with Him and other Christians for all eternity. What a special reunion day that will be!

Check the statements that most closely reflect your current feelings. (These are for personal reflection, not group discussion).

____I have questions on this topic and would like more information.

____I have a clearer understanding of life after death following this study and am thankful there will be a resurrection at the coming of Jesus.

____I want to be ready to meet Jesus at His second coming.

____I have never been baptized and would like to be in the near future. (Tell your group leader.)

____Other_____

Alone With God

This week after you have studied a passage of Scripture, sit quietly for 5-10 minutes thinking about what you have read. Allow God to speak to the needs of your life.

17

Sin—Forever Gone

GROUP LIFE

Growing Together—Decisions

Have you ever known someone who had difficulty making decisions? Maybe this person loved someone and dated for a long time but was not sure if they should get married. There was always the possibility they would each meet someone later that they loved more. Or maybe this person passes up a job opportunity or promising financial investment. Such a person misses out on many opportunities in life.

Decisions and change can be difficult. Each of these guides includes several response questions to help you reflect on the question of how the material studied impacts your personal life. As you and others of your group make decisions, be supportive of one another. Pray together, give verbal support, and demonstrate acceptance by your actions.

Sharing Life

As one reads the Gospels, it is clear that when Jesus came in contact with people, their lives were changed. In considering your own life, who, besides Jesus, has impacted you the most, and why?

SCRIPTURE AND LIFE

WHAT JESUS SAID ABOUT HELL

"And do not fear those who kill the body but cannot kill the soul. But rather fear Him who is able to destroy both soul and body in hell."—Matthew 10:28

As you study, be thinking about the LifeQuest questions:
- What does this topic tell me about God?
- What difference does this topic make in my daily life?
- How does this topic help me in my relationship with Jesus?

Many people have written theories concerning the events following the second coming of Jesus to this earth. One item most biblical scholars agree on is that Jesus will return and that eternal life will be given to God's people. However, the Bible does speak about the order of events.

Revelation, in chapters 16-22, discusses the final scenes of earth's history. Revelation 16:13 mentions three powers that will arise and oppose Jesus. These are the dragon, the beast, and the false prophet. (In prophecy the dragon represents Satan [Revelation 20:2]; the beast and false prophet are apostate Christianity. Details concerning the identities of these powers and their characteristics is another complete study.) Chapters 17-19 deal with the actions and demise of the beast power and false prophet. In Revelation 19:19 the three powers opposing Jesus organize themselves to fight Him at His coming. The outcome of Christ's coming is that sin and sinners are eventually destroyed. What follows in chapter 20 are the events of the millennium and descriptions of what happens to the dragon (Satan) at Christ's coming. The term *millennium* means "a thousand years."

❑ Read Revelation 20:1-15. What is the meaning and significance of the bottomless pit, the key, and the great chain? (verses 1-3)

_____

Why is Satan bound to the earth for a thousand years?

_____

❑   Identify and discuss the groups of people referred to in this passage (verses 4-6). Keep in mind that prior to Jesus' coming there are four groups of human beings—righteous living, righteous dead, wicked living, and wicked dead. (See 1 Thessalonians 4:13-18; 1 Corinthians 15:20-24.)

_____

◆   Verse 4 refers to a judgment. What is it, and why does it occur?

_____

◆   Verse 5 mentions a "first resurrection," which implies at least a second resurrection. Also, it mentions that the dead would live again at the end of the thousand years. Verse 6 mentions a second death for them. Discuss and outline in order the events as described so far (verses 1-6). _____

_____

_____

❑   Read verses 7-10. The previous verses (1-6) discussed Satan being released and deceiving nations, a second resurrection, and a second death. Do you see these events referred to in verses 7-10? If not, what *is* being referred to, in your opinion?

_____

❑   Verses 11-15 summarize the fact that anyone whose name is not found in the Book of Life is cast into the lake of fire—the second death. As you think about the events described, how do you feel?

___afraid   ___peace and trust in God
___ready for the judgment   even though some things
___angry with God   are hard to understand
___not ready for the judgment   ___ other _____

❑   Now that your study of chapter 20 is complete, summarize the events described that need to be added to your previous summary. (If you would like, make a chart showing all the events studied in this lesson.)_____

❑ There are two basic viewpoints on the lake of fire known as hell. One is that the fire never ceases burning. A second view is that the fire is not eternal in its burning but in its consequences. That is, the wicked are eternally destroyed and the righteous receive eternal life. Romans 6:23 helps clarify which view is correct: "For the wages of sin is death, but the gift of God is eternal life in Christ Jesus our Lord." Life and death are contrasted here, showing that those who choose Jesus receive eternal life rather than death. The following Scriptures assist in clarifying the issue.

◆ **The completeness of the destruction of sinners.** Read and discuss the fate of sinners and sin. Malachi 4:1, 3; 2 Thessalonians 1:9, 10; 2 Peter 3:10-13; Psalm 92:7._____

_____

◆ **Everlasting or eternal punishment.** Read and discuss the following passages and the biblical use of the words *eternal* or *everlasting*.

■ Sodom and Gommorah: Jude 7 and 2 Peter 2:6

■ Jerusalem (fire "shall not be quenched"). Jeremiah 17:27; 25:9-12; 2 Chronicles 36:19-21.

■ Discuss each Scripture in reference to the fire being eternal in results and consequences vs. being an eternal punishment. Everlasting punishment (Matthew 25:45, 46); eternal redemption (Hebrews 9:11, 12); and eternal judgment (Hebrews 6:1, 2).

◆ **Forever.** Read and compare the use of *forever* in these passages: Exodus 21:5-6; 1 Samuel 1:22; Jonah 2:6; Philemon 15, 16. Discuss how the term *forever* as used in these passages sheds light on the meaning of forever and ever.

◆ Discuss how God's love is seen in the destruction of sin and sinners.

❏ LIFEQUEST—Thoughtfully review these questions:
  ◼ What does this topic tell me about God?
  ◼ What difference does this topic make in my daily life?
  ◼ How does this topic help me in my relationship with Jesus?

APPLICATION TO LIFE

Real Life

The illustration on the window poster jumped out at the shoppers as they walked by the storefront. The poster graphically portrayed a man surrounded by flames, with his arms outstretched upward. As the flames licked at his flesh, the man's face was contorted in agony and pain. The headline was followed by an address advertising a series of meetings in a local church. One can only imagine the variety of opinions and ideas the poster generated in the mind of the person on the street.

From a young age, many children in America become aware of adult discussions about heaven and hell. Theories vary from those based on speculation and what one has been told, to theories that are biblically supported. In discussing hell, some concentrate on the question of how God can be loving and still destroy sin and sinners.

Many Christians have spent hours assisting people as they wrestle with this issue. The difficult concepts of hell and God's character need to be understood, because misunderstanding prevents some from making a decision to become active Christians.

A group could spend considerable time on the subject, but a few summary points are as follows. God wants His relationship with mankind to be a relationship based upon love and man's free choice. He knows that force inhibits true relationships. Sin entered in the beginning because God allowed Lucifer and the angels freedom of choice to have a relationship with Him or not to have one. The same option was given to Adam and Eve in the Garden of Eden and has been offered to everyone since that time. God also has told His created beings in advance what the results of their choice will be. One choice results in eternal life; the other in eternal death. This choice is also yours. God provides a way of escape through Jesus Christ, because He does not want anyone to be destroyed. People choose, and God provides the means to fulfill their choice. Once sin is obliterated, there will never again be any sin or its results upon the earth. All will be in perfect harmony.

Your Turn

The subject of the destruction of sin and sinners is one that is simultaneously sad and joyous. Sad because of the loss of life; joyous because sin will cease to exist. Some aspects of this subject are difficult to understand because man is attempting to understand God. Finite man cannot fully comprehend the infinite.

What one chooses to do with God's invitation to develop a relationship with Him will chart his or her final destiny. God's Word is true, and events will occur just as the Bible has stated. The question is, what will be your choice?

Check the statements that most closely reflect your current feelings. (These are for personal reflection, not group discussion.)

___ I would like more information on the topic of hell and the millennium.

___ I accept Jesus as Lord and Saviour of my life and desire to spend eternity with Him.

___ I believe that God is fair and loving because He gives people the choice of determining their eternal destiny.

___ Please pray for me that I will make the correct choices in my life.

___ Other_____

Alone With God

Some time this week, find a quiet place in your house and read John 3:14-17. As you read the verses, concentrate on the thought that God wants everyone saved. What do you find in these verses that expresses to you God's love and plan for man?

18

Forever Young

GROUP LIFE

Growing Together—Change and Group Life

One of the goals of your group is to arrive at a better understanding of the Bible. As a member contemplates Scripture and possible life changes, other members should not apply pressure. Group members should provide support and encouragement, and pray for the one considering change. In fact, members should make sure that no one in the group feels pressured or like they are "second class" because of their choices.

Acceptance does not mean that other group members agree with everything a person may say or do. Mutual respect is the key ingredient. The Holy Spirit will guide each person to make decisions when he or she is ready.

Sharing Life

A popular saying has it that "no man is an island." That is, everyone is impacted by someone or something. What event has impacted your life the most?

SCRIPTURE AND LIFE

WHAT JESUS SAID ABOUT HEAVEN

"In My Father's house are many mansions; if it were not so, I would have told you. I go to prepare a place for you. And if I go and prepare a place for you, I will come again and receive you to Myself, that where I am, there you may be also."—John 14:2, 3

As you study, be thinking about the LifeQuest questions:

■ What does this topic tell me about God?

■ What difference does this topic make in my daily life?

■ How does this topic help me in my relationship with Jesus?

As children, when we thought of heaven, it was usually about lions, bears, and tigers providing "horseback rides." As adults, the list includes wondering where we will live, what we will do, whom we will know, and what it will be like to be with Jesus.

Following the cleansing of the earth from sin as described in Revelation 20, John discusses life in a new heaven and earth.

❑ Read Revelation 21:1-8. In what sense are heaven and earth made new?

_____

◆ Why do you think the city is called "New Jerusalem"? Who are the residents of the New Jerusalem?

_____

◆ What has caused you mourning, crying, or pain this past year? What does it mean to you to know that pain as we must now experience it will be gone?_____

◆ What do you think it will be like living without fear, pain, death, or tears—and being continually with Jesus?

___fantastic   ___come quickly, Lord Jesus
___indescribable   ___other _____
___scares me

◆ Why is there no need for a temple in the New Jerusalem?
(verse 22)_____

❑ Read Revelation 21:9-27. Discuss the New Jerusalem as a *home environment*. Discuss and list the physical aspects of the city.

    appearance _____

    size of city, wall, etc. _____

    food and water supplies _____

    medical _____

    other items of interest _____

◆ *Physical appearance.* The description of Jesus' resurrected body in John 20:24-29, John 21, and Luke 24:30, 31, and 35 tells us something about what our bodies will be like in heaven. What insights do you find in these verses?_____
_____

❑ The prophet Isaiah, in Isaiah 35:5, 6; 65:17-25; 66:22, 23, adds other details to the picture. One must remember that these passages describes what God would have done for Israel if they had fulfilled God's purpose. Since Israel failed, the prophecy will be fulfilled in principle for the new heaven and new earth, but not in every detail. What do these passages add to your understanding of the new heaven and new earth?_____
_____

In these verses, what applies to Israel of old and what applies to the new earth? _____
_____

In this life, we sometimes say, "All good things come to an end." But in the new earth, the good things are eternally ours. As John says in Revelation 11:15, "The kingdom of the world has become the kingdom of our Lord and of his Christ, and he will reign forever and ever!"

❏ **LIFEQUEST**—Thoughtfully review these questions:
- ■ What does this topic tell me about God?
- ■ What difference does this topic make in my daily life?
- ■ How does this topic help me in my relationship with Jesus?

APPLICATION TO LIFE

Real Life

Bob and Fred were college roommates. One night they were relaxing on their beds, talking about heaven. The two young men were discussing what they knew about heaven and were speculating about the rest. After a half hour, the discussion changed to the things on this earth that they enjoyed and looked forward to in the future that might not be in heaven.

Fred stated that he would be disappointed if he were not able to graduate from college, be married and raise a family, and start a career before Jesus returned to this earth. He said he wanted Jesus to come, but not for a few years. Bob responded by saying that life did not always turn out the way one plans. If Fred could look into the future, he might desire Jesus to come instead of experiencing his plans on earth.

Later, Fred's plans were partially realized, but not as he had envisioned. He married and lived through some very stressful years that almost ended in divorce. His career bottomed out, and he found himself starting over with a young family. This added financial and personal stress to his life. Several friends and family members died, which caused special relationships to end. Fifteen years later, as Fred and Bob reflected on their lives since college, it was obvious to both of them that this life is filled with hurt, struggles, and disappointments.

Bob's life had been somewhat more positive than Fred's. However, a loss of health had significantly altered his enjoyment of life at a young age. As Bob read in the Bible about a new earth where he would have renewed vitality forever, he quoted the words of Revelation, along with the disciple John: "Even so, come quickly, Lord Jesus."

Your Turn

There are bright and enjoyable moments in life, but most would agree that sadness and tragedy are a portion of this life's experience. The biblical description of heaven makes us want Jesus to come and end this era of life.

If you are struggling as you consider the benefits of heaven over this earth, think about the following. Do you want people to die and have tragic accidents? In heaven there will be no accidents or death. Do you want people to have poor health and pain? In heaven everyone will have the vitality of youth. Do you want people to have happy family relationships? In heaven relationships will all be positive. Heaven will contain the best of this earth plus added benefits and pleasures. Why? Because God is love.

Check the statements that most closely reflect your current feelings. (These are for personal reflections, not group discussion).

___I would like more information about heaven.
___I want to go to heaven when Jesus comes again.
___I accept Jesus as Lord and Saviour of my life.
___Other_____

Alone With God

Ask God to assist you in enjoying life now but to look forward to a more enjoyable life at the second coming of Jesus. As you grow in your spiritual relationship, many of these issues will continue to come into perspective.

19

Symbols of Salvation

GROUP LIFE

Growing Together—Affirmation

Affirmation is the process of encouraging and strengthening someone, to help him or her grow and develop. A friend of mine shared a biblical insight with me concerning affirmation.

The story takes place in the book of Judges. The Midianites are oppressing Israel. Gideon is threshing wheat in the winepress to hide it from the Midianites. God appears to him and says, "The Lord is with you, you mighty man of valor!" Gideon goes on to question whether God is really with Israel because of what has happened. God, however, had great plans for Gideon and tells him those plans by words of affirmation. God says to a man hiding in a winepress that he is a brave man. Instead of saying, "Why are you hiding? Don't you trust me?" God calls him a mighty man of valor. God affirms Gideon. He sees his potential and affirms him in a way that brings out the characteristic of valor.

Likewise, the members in your group are growing as individuals. Each has character-development needs. Words of encouragement and affirmation will help them grow as individuals and group members.

Sharing Life

Following the death of Jesus, the disciples reflected on some of the key events and statements of Jesus that meant the most to them. In your experience, what is one of your happiest memories?

SCRIPTURE AND LIFE

WHAT JESUS SAID ABOUT SALVATION

"And as Moses lifted up the serpent in the wilderness, even so must the Son of Man be lifted up, 'that whoever believes in Him should not perish but have eternal life.'"—John 3:14, 15

As you study, be thinking about the LifeQuest questions:

■ What does this topic tell me about God?

■ What difference does this topic make in my daily life?

■ How does this topic help me in my relationship with Jesus?

It is Friday evening on Golgotha's hill. Darkness has put a covering over the city of Jerusalem. The priest is ready to offer the lamb for the evening sacrifice. As the knife is poised, ready to end the life of its bleating victim, an earthquake rumbles through the city. The ground heaves and rolls; the lamb escapes from the priest's arms; Jesus cries out, "It is finished"—causing the veil of the temple "to be torn in two from top to bottom" (Matthew 27:51). The sacrifice of Jesus on the cross has ended the significance of the sanctuary service.

Have you ever wondered why the curtain was torn in the temple? What did it mean? The reason is simple, once we understand the issues. God instructed Moses (Exodus 25:8) to build a sanctuary or temple where He could dwell and where the Israelites would conduct religious services. Hebrews 9:23, 24 says that Moses' tabernacle was "a copy of the things in the heavens." Later, King David designed a permanent temple in Jerusalem, which was built by his son, King Solomon.

This study guide will have two parts. Part one will summarize the physical aspects of the sanctuary and their meaning. Part two will explore the message of the sanctuary as described in the book of Hebrews.

The Sanctuary

Exodus 25-27; 31:1-11; 35:4 through 40:38 discusses the building of the sanctuary. Because of the length of the chapters, read only the following verses and discuss/list the items that make up the physical aspects of the sanctuary. You might only have time to list the items of furniture and discuss the meaning of two or three during your group time.

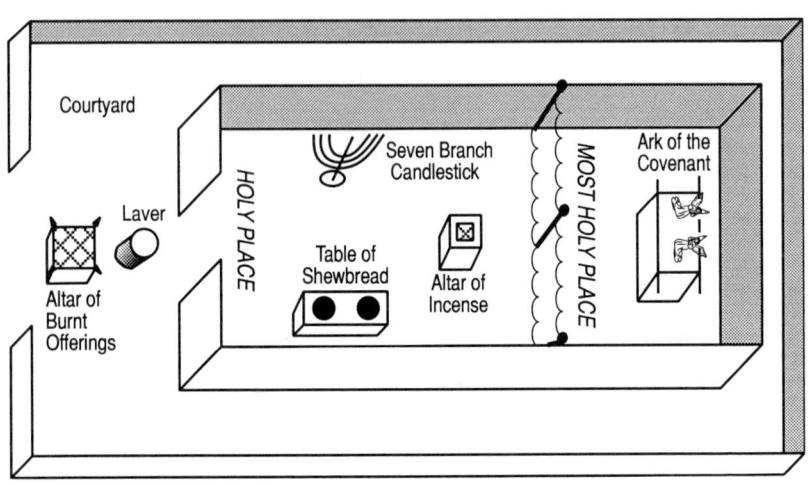

◆   Exodus 25:10-22. _____
What is the "testimony" God was going to give to Moses? What is the significance of the "testimony" being in the ark and of the top being called the "mercy seat"? _____

◆   Exodus 25:23, 24, 30. _____
Also read John 6:31-35; Matthew 26:26. Discuss how these verses assist in understanding the bread and its purpose. _____

_____

◆   Exodus 25:31-33. _____

Also read John 1:4, 5; 1 John 1:5-7. Discuss the meaning of this piece of furniture._____

_____

◆   Exodus 26:1, 30-37. _____

To assist in understanding the meaning of these verses, read also Exodus 34:29-35._____

_____

◆ Exodus 30:1, 34-38. _____

Also read Psalm 141:1, 2 and discuss the relationship and significance of this piece of furniture._____

_____

◆ Exodus 27:1; 29:38, 39. _____
Also read and discuss Matthew 20:28, Romans 5:6, and John 1:29 for insight and comparison._____

_____

◆ Exodus 27:9-19. _____

Discuss the purpose of the courtyard._____

_____

◆ Exodus 30:17-21. _____
Also read Acts 22:16 and John 13:12-17, and then discuss the insights these passages give you._____

_____

◆ Exodus 30:22-25. _____
What is the meaning of "holy"? What makes the oil holy?_____

_____

◆ Leviticus 16:34 mentions the "atonement." Discuss the meaning of the word *atonement*. During your personal daily study time, read Leviticus 16 to understand the details of the Day of Atonement.

❑ Which of the pieces of furniture and other items just studied mean the most to you, and why?_____

___Ark/Mercy Seat   ___Lampstand
___Veil   ___Laver
___Most Holy Place   ___Altar of Burnt Offering
___Holy Place   ___Oil
___Altar of Incense   ___Courtyard/Tabernacle
___Table of Shewbread

The Meaning of the Sanctuary

As previously mentioned, the earthly sanctuary was a copy of the one in heaven. The purpose of the sanctuary on earth was to point to the coming Saviour, who would provide forgiveness and eternal life. The sanctuary services pointed to His coming the first time to this earth.

❑ Hebrews 8:1-6. Why was it necessary to have a sanctuary in heaven and a copy of it on the earth?_____

◆ What is the significance of Jesus being our High Priest?

❑ Read Hebrews 9:1-28. Verses 6 and 7 refer to two services the priests performed. One was daily, the other once a year. Discuss how Christ's blood (vss. 11, 12) fulfilled these services.

◆ In your opinion, what is the theme message of verses 23-28?

❑ As you have studied these Scriptures, it has become obvious that there was significant planning and preparation by the Godhead to acquaint people with Jesus and His sacrifice. This is a message of restoration—man and God being reunited together in a relationship of love and forgiveness—and both looking forward to experiencing God's plan of eternal life together. When you tell others that Jesus died for their sins, how do most react?

___excited	___gratitude
___interested	___hard to believe
___indifferent	___other

❑ Why do you think God used symbols to explain the plan of salvation and His love for mankind?

❑ LIFEQUEST—Thoughtfully review these questions:
  ■ What does this topic tell me about God?
  ■ What difference does this topic make in my daily life?
  ■ How does this topic help me in my relationship with Jesus?

APPLICATION TO LIFE

Real Life

"I do not believe that the Old Testament has meaning today. It is simply a history of the Israelites. The New Testament contains God's message for the church." So said Sarah in responding to the group leader's comment that a teaching in the Old Testament had application for twentieth-century Christians.

Some relate to the Old Testament as Sarah did. But when this view is taken, much of the message of God is lost.

One illustration of the blending of the Old and New Testaments is seen in the completed study on Hebrews 9. There is unity in God's theme of salvation as seen in Scripture. In order to help Sarah understand this point, her group leader used a study such as the one just completed to assist her. As Sarah studied, she realized that the source of many texts in the New Testament is the Old Testament. As in Hebrews 9, the sanctuary reference demonstrates a link between the heavenly sanctuary, the Old Testament sanctuary, and the plan of redemption through Jesus Christ. Ignoring the Old Testament account eliminates much of what we can learn about the plan of salvation.

Your Turn

This study has been about what the sanctuary tells us about Jesus. Jesus as our High Priest offered Himself as our sacrifice so that each person living on the earth could have forgiveness of sins. The decision to accept Jesus is the most important decision anyone can ever make.

Check the statements that most closely reflect your current feelings. (These are for personal reflection, not group discussion.)

____I have accepted Jesus as Saviour and Lord of my life and desire to recommit my life to Him.

____I accept Jesus as Saviour and Lord of my life. I desire to follow Him completely.

____ I am thankful for the complete message given in both the Old and New Testaments.

____Other_____

Alone With God

A Scripture which reflects this week's study is found in Romans 6:23. If you have not memorized it, sometime this week commit it to memory: "For the wages of sin is death, but the gift of God is eternal life in Christ Jesus our Lord."

20

The Future Predicted

GROUP LIFE

Growing Together—Trust and Confidence

In order to build trust among group members, it is necessary to discuss the need for acceptance. After this is done, there are two steps that will demonstrate to the group that trust is a part of group life. The first is to express feelings of acceptance and support for any person who shares openly with the group. This does not necessarily mean that you agree with the one sharing, but assures the person that his or her opinions do not hurt your relationship. The second step is to model your belief that the group is a safe environment by expressing your own personal feelings and opinions openly.

Sharing Life

As we think about Jesus' life, certain events are always more meaningful to us than others, depending upon our own life experience. What event in Christ's life means the most to you, and why?

SCRIPTURE AND LIFE

WHAT JESUS SAID ABOUT JUDGMENT

"For the Father judges no one, but has committed all judgment to the Son, that all should honor the Son, just as they honor the Father." John 5:22, 23.

As you study, be thinking about the LifeQuest questions:

■ What does this topic tell me about God?

■ What difference does this topic make in my daily life?

■ How does this topic help me in my relationship with Jesus?

The study guide entitled "Symbols of Salvation" discussed the Old Testament sanctuary services and their meaning and importance to salvation. An in-depth study of the Old Testament services in Exodus and in Hebrews revealed two events—the daily services, and the Day of Atonement, which occurred once a year and was known as cleansing or purifying the sanctuary from sin.

What this meant was that the daily services symbolized the forgiveness of sins for the people—their sins were transferred to the sanctuary through the sacrifices and offerings, just as Jesus took our sins upon Him. Once a year (Day of Atonement—Leviticus 16 and 23) the sins were symbolically done away with forever, through a sacrifice representing Jesus and the sending into the wilderness of a goat representing Satan. This cleansed the sanctuary of all sins and purified it completely.

The Day of Atonement was a day when the sins of the children of Israel were declared cleansed because of their previous sacrifices for forgiveness (see Leviticus 16:16, 34). The people and the sanctuary were cleansed by the special service, and all was purified. This service pointed to the time following Jesus' sacrifice when:

■ The "pre-millennial" or "pre-Advent" judgment takes place. Before Jesus comes, those whose sins have been forgiven and whose names have been written in the Book of Life (Revelation 20:15) will be declared safe to save for eternity, and all record of their sins will be blotted out (Revelation 22:11, 12; Daniel 7:22; Matthew 25:31-34).

■ The banishment of the scapegoat to the wilderness symbolized Satan's millennial imprisonment on earth and the judgment of the wicked (Revelation 20:4).

■ The cleansed or purified sanctuary and camp represents the fire that destroys the wicked and cleanses the earth (Revelation 20:11-15).

Some biblical scholars describe these three events as "three judgment phases," or three steps to restoration. In summary, the first is when God reviews, with the universe, the names of those written in the Book of Life and declares them to have eternal life. The second is when, during the millennium, God reviews with the universe and the saved that those who didn't receive eternal life made their own decision—and that God is fair, just, and good. The third phase is when fire cleanses the earth and destroys sin, and the earth is restored.

A very important question is, When does this three-phase process begin? The Bible's answer is found in the book of Daniel.

Daniel records a vision he had about the history of the world. Various animals represented four major world empires—Babylon (lion), Medo-Persia (bear), Greece (leopard), and Rome (dreadful beast). Following these, the next world empire is to be the kingdom of Jesus (Daniel 7).

Daniel also learned that the fourth power would speak against God, attempt to change His law (Daniel 7:23-25). After this fourth kingdom, however, God will intervene and establish His kingdom (vss. 26-28).

Daniel was troubled (vs. 28) and asked God (8:13) how long it would be until the apostate power would be overthrown and His kingdom reestablished. The answer comes in verse 14: "And he said to me, 'For two thousand three hundred days; then the sanctuary shall be cleansed.'"

Notice the use of the word *cleansed* as we have previously studied it. The question being asked is, "When is the first phase of judgment to begin?" Or, "When does the final process of God's restoration of His people begin?" It is important to note that the angel tells Daniel that "the vision refers to the time of the end." (8:16, 17). In verse 27, Daniel is troubled and doesn't clearly understand the vision —and faints. In chapter 9, as Daniel prays, God sends an angel to interpret his vision.

Three points will help us understand the angel's answer to Daniel:

■ The vision is at the time of the end.

■ Since the earthly sanctuary system ceased when Jesus died on the cross, and since Daniel's prophecy goes to the end of time, Daniel's prophecy must apply to God's heavenly sanctuary.

■ A vital clue in understanding this vision is that time in prophecy is usually symbolic (read Ezekiel 4:6; Numbers 14:34).

Discuss how these passages may help in understanding Daniel's prophecy of the 2300 days.

❑ Read Daniel 9:24-27. Discuss each part of this passage to identify what is being said.

Verse 24:

■ Seventy weeks = _____
■ Your people = _____
■ Holy city = _____
■ Finish transgression, etc. = _____

Verse 25:

■ Why did Jerusalem need to be restored and rebuilt? (See Daniel 1:1; Jeremiah 29:10; and Ezra 1:1-4). The rebuilding process was futile until the time of Artaxerxes (Ezra 7). The time of the decree in Ezra 7 is the autumn of 457 B.C._____

_____

■ Who is Messiah the Prince? (John 1:29-36, 41)_____

_____

■ Discuss and calculate the seven-week and sixty-two-week periods based upon what you have learned._____

_____

Verse 26:

■ "Messiah shall be cut off" means: (See Matthew 27:35, 50.)

_____

■ "People of the Prince will come and destroy the city and sanctuary" means: (See Matthew 24:1-3.)

_____

Verse 27:

Refers to same time period as verse 26. What has just been studied is Gabriel's answer to Daniel concerning the 2300-day prophecy. As can be seen, it is a two-part answer. The beginning date is given for (1) a 490-year period for the Jews to do God's will and (2) the same date begins the 2300 days, which signifies when the sanctuary is to be cleansed. The following chart outlines what has been studied.

TIME OF THE END

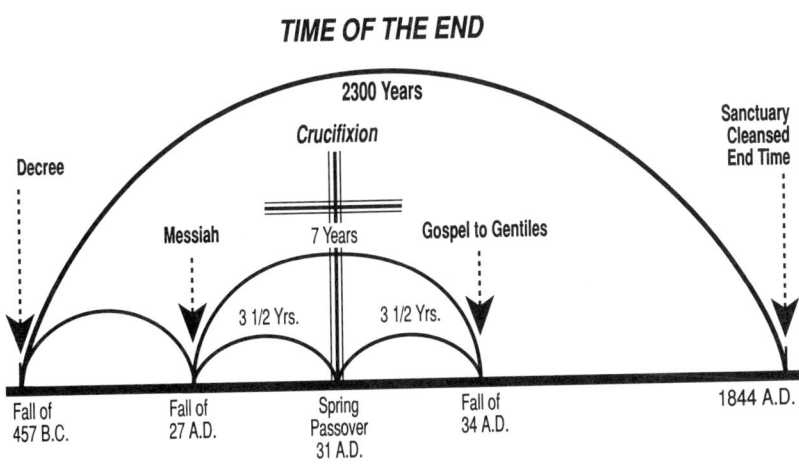

- ■ Apply each scripture to a date on the chart.
- ■ Discuss and answer each other's questions.

Based upon what has just been studied, the Bible pinpoints the "cleansing of the sanctuary" as beginning in A.D. 1844. This means that since 1844, the beginning phase of the judgment has been taking place!

❑ **LIFEQUEST**—Thoughtfully review these questions:
- ■ What does this topic tell me about God?
- ■ What difference does this topic make in my daily life?
- ■ How does this topic help me in my relationship with Jesus?

APPLICATION TO LIFE

Real Life

As Wayne entered his teen years, he began to question how he could be certain that the Bible was accurate and that God did exist. About this time, he began to lose interest in church attendance. His mother said, "OK, if you stay home from church, you must spend some time studying your Bible." He thought that was a good trade-off and agreed.

Wayne decided to complete some study guides on the books of Daniel and Revelation. As he studied the prophecies, he began to realize the existence of God. He investigated and discovered that the events portrayed were forecast before they occurred. After studying Daniel 2 on the history of world kingdoms and Daniel 9 on the subject of the 2300 days, he was convinced God did exist and that the Bible was the Word of God.

Your Turn

Many Christians are afraid of the judgment. They think that the judgment means that their good works are stacked up against their bad deeds—and hopefully, the "good works" stack is taller! We can say thank you to God that this is not how the judgment is conducted.

When your name comes up in the judgment, the question asked will be, "What has this person done with Jesus? Has he or she chosen to have Jesus forgive his or her sins?" If the answer is yes, then it will be declared that you are safe to save for eternity. The judgment is *Good News!*

Check the statements that most closely reflect your current feelings. (These are for personal reflection, not group discussion.)

_____ I accept Jesus as Lord and Saviour of my life.
_____ I want to be ready to meet Jesus when He returns to this earth.
_____ I am thankful that the judgment is good news for the Christian!
_____ I recommit my life to Jesus with the intent and desire to follow Him each day of my life.
_____ Other_____

Alone With God

Take time this week to prayerfully review your life. Is there an attitude, action, or activity that you need to release to Jesus? Are you completely surrendered to Him?

21

Symbols of Commitment

GROUP LIFE

Growing Together—Group Support

The life of a group member may at times be affected by pressures and conflicts at work or home—or the topic being studied may cause tension or uneasiness. When these situations occur, members may react in different ways. They may withdraw or stop coming to the group. They may come but not participate—or they may try to dominate the conversation (when they normally do not) or begin to be critical.

When there are behavioral changes in a fellow group member, be understanding of them. As a group member, do not wait for others to take the lead before you minister to another.

Sharing Life

It is intriguing to most people to understand their backgrounds and ancestry. What is the religious or denominational background of your parents and earlier ancestors—or what church did you attend as a child?

SCRIPTURE AND LIFE

> ## WHAT JESUS SAID ABOUT STEWARDSHIP OF LIFE
>
> "But seek first the kingdom of God and His righteousness, and all these things shall be added to you."—Matthew 6:33
>
> *As you study, be thinking about the LifeQuest questions:*
> - What does this topic tell me about God?
> - What difference does this topic make in my daily life?
> - How does this topic help me in my relationship with Jesus?

Life is made up of commitments. These commitments may include wedding vows, house payments, acceptance of a job responsibility, etc.

In addition, a Christian life means commitment—giving of ourselves and accepting Jesus and His plan for our lives. Acceptance of God's plan for us means that we become partners with God. This study will assist in understanding our responsibility in a relationship with Jesus.

❑ Read the following Scriptures and discuss (a) man's responsibility to God, and (b) God's response to man. Psalm 24:1; 1 Corinthians 6:19, 20; 1 Corinthians 3:21 - 4:2.

What areas of life are we supposed to manage for God?

❑ Life consists of at least five basic areas. These areas are our bodies, abilities, time, material possessions, and the world around us—or environment. Let's briefly review each area.

◆ **Stewardship of the Body**
Read these texts and discuss a person's responsibility for his or her physical well being. 1 Corinthians 6:19, 20; 3:16, 17; 10:31; 3 John 2, 3. (The next study guide discusses God's plan for

healthy living.) What areas of health and physical well-being do you think apply to the principles presented?_____

_____

◆ **Stewardship of Abilities**
Read these texts and discuss a person's responsibility to God for abilities and talents. 1 Corinthians 12:1, 4-7; Matthew 25:14-30.

How do you use the abilities God has given you?

___I hide them—I'm shy   ___volunteer to use them
___use them gladly   ___other_____
___quietly fulfill my duties

◆ **Stewardship of Time**
Read these texts and discuss a person's responsibility to God in the use of time. Colossians 3:23, 24; Exodus 20:8-11. For the Christian, can time be divided between secular and sacred—or is all time sacred?_____

_____

◆ **Stewardship of Material Possessions**
In the Garden of Eden, Adam and Eve were given a restriction to show their commitment to God, which was not to eat of the tree of the knowledge of good and evil. After sin entered, God wanted to remind us that He is the one who gives blessings and wealth, as He stated in Deuteronomy 8:18. The symbol of the Christian's recognition of God's ownership is tithe and offerings. Select several texts and discuss them. Leviticus 27:30-32; Numbers 18:21, 24; Malachi 3:8-12; Matthew 23:23, 24; Matthew 6:19-21; 2 Corinthians 9:6, 7; Psalm 96:7-9.

a. Define tithe and offerings. _____
b. Purpose and use of the tithe and offerings. _____

_____

c. God's promise to those who are faithful in tithes and offer
    ings. _____

◆ **Stewardship of the Environment**

Another area God has entrusted to His people is the care of the
environment He has provided. Read Genesis 2:15, 19, 20, which
describes the responsibility God gave Adam in the beginning.
What was Adam's role in caring for the garden?_____

_____

What should be a Christian's role in dealing with environmental
problems—personal and political?

___ not to litter	___organize community projects
___ pick up litter	___teach others to be aware of our
___ become an activist for	duty
the environment	___other _____

❏ **LIFEQUEST**—Thoughtfully review these questions:
  ■ What does this topic tell me about God?
  ■ What difference does this topic make in my daily life?
  ■ How does this topic help me in my relationship with Jesus?

APPLICATION TO LIFE

Real Life

John could tell that Brian was troubled following the study on the
topic of tithe and offerings. When he questioned Brian, John discovered
that Brian was short almost every month in having enough money to
pay his bills. In fact, he had even considered acquiring a second job. It
seemed almost impossible to return to God ten percent of his income,
plus an offering.

John shared two basic points with Brian. He told him to analyze his
budget to determine if there were areas that could be adjusted to provide
finances for tithe. He also directed Brian's attention to the promises God

makes about giving a special blessing to those who choose to follow the Scriptural directions concerning tithing. God says to put Him to the test on this matter, and Brian was encouraged to accept the challenge.

As Brian analyzed his budget, he decided that if he quit smoking and went out to dinner one less time a month and adjusted his car payment, he should be able almost to cover the necessary funding for his tithe and offerings. He knew it would be difficult at first but that God would assist him.

Your Turn

If you have never had tithe and offerings as part of your personal budget, it is common to have concerns similar to Brian's. Every Christian has to make the decision to return tithes and offerings—or not to do so—at some time in life. For most, it is an adjustment at first that takes some careful planning. Once it is part of your budget, over time it simply becomes a normal budget item. God knew it would be a difficult adjustment for some people. That is why He provided the Scripture that says to put His promise to the test on this issue.

If you are contemplating what you will do with this teaching of Scripture, remember that with God's assistance, everything is possible.

Check the statements that most closely reflect your current feelings. (These are for personal reflection not group discussion.)

___ I would like additional information on this topic. Pray for me.
___ I choose to form a partnership with God concerning the five areas I studied in this study guide.
___ I have decided to return to God on a regular basis the tithe and offerings from the income He provides for me.
___ Other_____

Alone With God

As you pray and think about making stewardship a part of your lifestyle, ask a fellow Christian about how this teaching has impacted his or her life. If you do not know someone to ask, your group leader would probably be more than willing to talk with you.

22

Life At Its Best

GROUP LIFE

Growing Together—Service and the Group Member

The purpose of the church and of your group is not only to encourage personal growth but to prepare members to serve others. The introductory part of each study guide has focused on how the group can be more effective as a unit. As members of your group grow spiritually, the group should spend some time discussing how each of you can share with others what Jesus has done for you.

As each of your group members grow in Jesus and are ministered to by the group, they in turn should reach out to others outside of the group to assist them in their lives.

Sharing Life

Experience has shown us that within a few days after moving into a new neighborhood or starting a new job, we make new friends who eventually become close acquaintances. Share how you met one of your closest friends—or how you met your best friend?

SCRIPTURE AND LIFE

WHAT JESUS SAID ABOUT LIFESTYLE

". . . I have come that they may have life, and that they may have it more abundantly."—John 10:10

As you study, be thinking about the LifeQuest questions:

■ What does this topic tell me about God?

■ What difference does this topic make in my daily life?

■ How does this topic help me in my relationship with Jesus?

Have you noticed the lifestyle and behavior of people in love? They do special things for one another and are eager to please the other person. Likewise, the lifestyle of a follower of God should be a response to God's love and His gift of salvation. A Christian will develop a particular lifestyle, not to earn God's love, but because of a love for God.

❑ Read Romans 12:1, 2 and John 17:15, 16, and discuss the following questions.

◆ Is it possible for a Christian to be both in the world and yet separate from it? If someone answers "yes," discuss how this is possible.   ___Yes   ___No   ___Not Sure

◆ How should the Christian lifestyle differ from that of the world? _____

◆ When Jesus lived on this earth, He was called a "glutton and a drunkard" (Matthew 11:19), though He was not guilty of sin. What does this mean to you?

___He associated with beer drinkers and party-goers but didn't drink.

___He cared about people no matter who they were and what type of lifestyle they lived.

___Christians should have friends who do not profess Christianity.

___Jesus should have been more careful about His associates.

___Be careful not to give a bad image.

___Other _____

❏ Read the following texts and discuss what they say to you concerning principles of choosing appropriate behavior. Consider both specific activities and overall lifestyle. 1 Corinthians 6:19, 20; 10:31; Philippians 4:8. (Also consider the texts from the previous page.)

_____

_____

Apply the principles you have just listed to the following items.

◆ work and rest _____

◆ movies, television, videos _____

◆ books and magazines _____

◆ nonprescription drugs _____

◆ tobacco _____

◆ alcoholic beverages _____

◆ radio, music _____

❏ In the Scriptures, God gives explicit instructions about diet. He is detailed about our eating habits. Discuss God's guidelines.

◆ What was man's original diet? Genesis 1:29 _____

◆ After the flood, what items were added to man's diet? Genesis 9:3, 4_____

◆ Into what classifications did God divide the animals? Genesis 7:2_____

Read Leviticus 11 and Deuteronomy 14 to discover what God classifies as clean and unclean foods. What is the principle you see God using to distinguish between clean and unclean? Why do you think God cares about what a person eats? List the guidelines and/or criteria for:

■ reptiles _____   ■ fish _____
■ birds _____   ■ mammals _____

❏ Another area in which God provides guidelines is in the matter of dress. Read 1 Timothy 2:9, 10 and 1 Peter 3:1-6, and discuss the principles outlined in these Scriptures. How should these principles apply to how a Christian dresses? Can adornment also include cars, houses, etc.?

Is it OK for different cultures and different eras of time to have different applications of the principles of modesty, dress, and adornment? Why?_____

As you can see from God's Word, He gives us counsel concerning broad areas of daily living. He does this because He is our Creator, and He loves us. As you contemplate what you have learned, remember one of the Scriptures in this lesson—"Therefore, whatever you eat or drink, or whatever you do, do all to the glory of God." 1 Corinthians 10:31.

❏ How do we avoid having our behavior become "works" rather than a response of love to God?

❏ LIFEQUEST—Thoughtfully review these questions:
   ■ What does this topic tell me about God?
   ■ What difference does this topic make in my daily life?
   ■ How does this topic help me in my relationship with Jesus?

APPLICATION TO LIFE

Real Life

Wayne appeared to be a healthy 29-year-old with a typical American lifestyle—fast-paced. He tried to squeeze jogging and other types of exercise in between business and travel. It never seemed as if he could get enough sleep. Whenever his schedule slowed down, his body seemed to slow down with it, and he would get a cold or flu. Wayne talked about living differently, but they were only good intentions in his mind until one day, following a heavy time of work stress, he developed a bronchial cold and felt very weak. Four weeks later another virus attacked his lungs in the form of pneumonia. Wayne, however, kept working, and within a short period of time, with a weakened body and immune system, he became nearly bedridden. He was only able to work for limited periods of time, and then he had to rest. The situation was bad enough that side effects prevailed for several months.

During this time, Wayne decided that changes had to be made. He realized from personal experience that God's principles of living are given for a reason, and he began changing his eating, working, resting, and exercise habits to coincide with a balanced lifestyle.

Your Turn

Many people know they should live differently, but find it difficult to discipline themselves to make the necessary changes. God is the solution. He promises that when we ask for assistance in changing our lifestyle to conform to Christian principles, He will give us the necessary assistance.

Check the statements that most closely reflect your current feelings. (These are for personal reflection, not group discussion.)

____I choose for God to be in control of every part of my life. I ask for His leading and power to help me make the necessary changes.

____Please pray for me as I continue to consider how to apply the principles in this lesson to my daily life.

____I accept Jesus as Lord and Saviour of my life.

____Other_____

Alone With God

True desire for successful lifestyle changes comes only when your life is yielded to Jesus. Consider the ways He has benefited your life this past week. Do not forget to thank and praise Him!

23

A Family Forever

GROUP LIFE

Growing Together—Tension and Conflict

A small group not only provides opportunities for personal growth and developing of friendships—it also provides an environment of discussion, in which disagreements may arise. Disagreement and tension are not always bad. If handled properly, they can bring understanding and growth. Through these times of tension, ideas expressed may not always be accepted, but the person expressing them should never feel rejected. Remember to smile often at one another and laugh together.

Experience in group life has revealed that if members express support for a person or for ideas they agree with, then when disagreeable issues arise, there is less tension. As a group, state verbally as one of your ground rules that it is OK to disagree.

Go ahead and have a lively discussion, remembering that love, acceptance, and forgiveness will make your group a safe and fun place to be!

Sharing Life

Loving one another will bond your group together. The Bible states that "God is love." What does this phrase mean to you?

SCRIPTURE AND LIFE

WHAT JESUS SAID ABOUT CHRISTIAN FELLOWSHIP

"Whoever desires to become great among you shall be your servant. And whoever of you desires to be first shall be slave of all."—Mark 10:43, 44

As you study, be thinking about the LifeQuest questions:
- What does this topic tell me about God?
- What difference does this topic make in my daily life?
- How does this topic help me in my relationship with Jesus?

When you are a Christian, you belong to a family. In fact, if your family experience has not been positive, as a Christian you are in for a special treat! Listen to these words of Paul: "For as the body is one and has many members, but all the members of the one body, being many, are one body, so also is Christ. For by one Spirit we were all baptized into one body . . . " 1 Corinthians 12:12, 13. The disciple John adds to this promise in John 1:12, 13 by saying, "But as many as received Him, to them He gave the right to become children of God, even to those who believe in His name: who were born, not of blood, nor of the will of the flesh, nor of the will of man, but of God."

There it is—through Jesus Christ you belong to a family that loves you and cares about you. Keep in mind that the family isn't perfect. Every member is still growing in Jesus. Each must have patience and forgiveness for the others!

❑ **Meeting with your family.** Read the following texts and discuss the benefits of Christians meeting for worship and Bible study. If you attend church or a small group, what personally means the most to you? Hebrews 10:24, 25; Psalm 133:1; Acts 2:42-47.

❑ **Communion service.** A previous study guide discussed how baptism is a symbol of beginning a new life in Jesus. Being placed under the water represents the burying of one's past and beginning a new life in Jesus. As a Christian, you will desire to renew your baptismal vow and acceptance of Jesus on a regular basis. God has provided a special service, involving water for cleansing, and bread and wine representing His sacrifice.

◆ *Service of Humility (Footwashing).* Read and discuss the following Scriptures. John 13:1-17. Review these verses and share what they say to you.

verses 3-5 _____

verses 6, 7 _____

verses 8-10 _____

verses 12-15 _____

verses 16, 17 _____

How does Jesus expect Christians today to follow His example?

___be available to meet needs   ___wash each other's feet

___show love and forgiveness   ___other _____

◆ *The Lord's Supper.* Read Matthew 26:26-30 and 1 Corinthians 11:23-34. Discuss the meaning of:

the bread _____

the fruit of the vine _____

unworthy manner _____

Jesus' promise in Matthew 26:29 _____

❑ **Anointing Service**

In times of sickness, God has given Christians a special service. (See James 5:13-18.) What spiritual preparation is necessary?

_____

What types of sickness are meant? _____

What do you think should determine when a person asks to be anointed with oil? _____

❏ **Children's Dedication.** Boys and girls are special to Jesus. Read Mark 10:13-16.

Jesus blessed the children. What does this tell us about Him?

_____

What is the characteristic in children, Jesus wants Christians to possess? (vs. 15) _____

How does God want Christians to respond today?

___put adults before children   ___dedicate children to Him
___put children before adults   ___other _____
___pray for children everyday

❏ How is God's love revealed in the special services studied in this guide?

❏ LIFEQUEST—Thoughtfully review these questions:
  ■ What does this topic tell me about God?
  ■ What difference does this topic make in my daily life?
  ■ How does this topic help me in my relationship with Jesus?

APPLICATION TO LIFE

Real Life

A pastor was visiting a small group to better understand how it was functioning and to become acquainted with the members. The group was studying prophecies of the Bible. The evening's study covered a detailed prophecy and was difficult for some of the members to understand. When the study was completed, one lady stated that it was interesting, but that there were a lot of areas of the prophecy she did not completely understand.

After closing prayer, the pastor spoke with the woman who had expressed her lack of understanding. She informed him that she did not belong to any church. Her Bible study group was her source of Christian fellowship and support for the needs of her life. She said that if she ever joined a church, it would be the one that most of her group belonged to, because if the rest of the church members were like her group members, the church would be very special.

God has provided these special services of the church as times of fellowship with Him and with one another. On these occasions Christians enter into a unique moment with God which enhances their relationship with Him. If a Christian does not participate in these special opportunities, his or her spiritual development will be dwarfed.

Your Turn

The fellowship of your group can be enhanced by participating in worship services, church dinners, social events, and related church activities which will provide fulfillment of relationship/social needs. As you grow spiritually, do not overlook the social benefits of church life. The benefits of church attendance, of corporate worship, expanded social fellowship, and—as previously mentioned—participation in the special services of the church, will assist all Christians in their spiritual and personal development.

Check the statements that most closely reflect your current feelings. (These are for personal reflection, not group discussion.)

___ I want to thank God for the experience of Christian fellowship.

___ I want to increase my fellowship with God and fellow Christians by beginning to attend church on a regular basis.

___ I accept the special services God has provided for Christians and choose to make them a part of my spiritual development in Jesus.

___ Other_____

Alone With God

In your spiritual development, there are probably several people who have especially influenced your life. Take a few moments this week to write them a note or to thank them personally for being used by God to make a difference in your life!

24

A Messenger
for Today

GROUP LIFE

Growing Together—Worship

Part of the established relationship of a small group each week includes fellowship, Bible study, and prayer together. In essence, you are involved in worship each week as your group meets. The worship experience you have found in your group can be enjoyed again each week by attending a worship service.

In Hebrews 10:25 (NIV), the apostle Paul shares the admonition for Christians "to not give up meeting together." One such meeting is your group. Another should be church attendance on Sabbath. If you are not already attending church, you should make it a matter of thought and prayer. On the Sabbath you can attend a study group, plus worship and fellowship with many other Christians like yourself.

Many group members have discovered that group attendance during the week and church attendance on Sabbath assists them greatly in Christian growth and development. If it seems new to you, try it for several weeks and see if your life is not improved.

Sharing Life

It is exciting for Christians to read about the life of Jesus and all the special things He did for others while on this earth. If you could choose something to be said at the end of your life describing what you did for others, what would you like that message to be?

SCRIPTURE AND LIFE

WHAT JESUS SAID ABOUT PROPHECY

"Do not think that I came to destroy the Law or the Prophets. I did not come to destroy but to fulfill."—Matthew 5:17

As you study, be thinking about the LifeQuest questions:

■ What does this topic tell me about God?

■ What difference does this topic make in my daily life?

■ How does this topic help me in my relationship with Jesus?

In the study guide on the topic of creation, we discovered that before sin, God spoke to Adam and Eve face to face. After sin, they hid from God in the garden because of their embarrassment and because sin and purity cannot exist together.

Following the entrance of sin, God communicated with His people in various ways. One of those methods was through prophets.

❑ Read the following texts and discuss God's use of people to convey His message.

◆ 2 Peter 1:21. Why do you think God chose one person over another to be a prophet? Were there special characteristics that made those chosen stand out above others?

◆ Amos 3:7. Why would God choose to speak through humans, when an angel could do a better job?

◆ Numbers 12:6. Read and discuss the key points.

Which of the following roles of the prophet do you think was most important? Why?

___assisted in founding the Christian church
___initiated the church's mission outreach
___united and protected the church
___encouraged the church
___gave warnings
___confirmed the faith and biblical teachings in difficult times.

❑ The book of Revelation states that God's last-day people ("rest of," "remnant"), will have the gift of prophecy.

◆ Read Ephesians 4:8, 11-16, where Paul explains that God gives the prophetic gift to His people. What do these verses say is the purpose of the gift of prophecy, along with the other gifts listed? _____

_____

◆ Read Peter's prediction of last-day prophets. Acts 2:14-21. What will be their role and function?_____

_____

◆ Read Revelation 12:17. What does the verse say about the people who are faithful to God? Read Revelation 19:10 to assist in understanding Revelation 12:17._____

_____

Does it surprise you that just prior to the second coming of Jesus God uses prophecy to guide His people?   ___Yes   ___No
Why?_____

❑ The Bible speaks of other prophets who did not write parts of the Bible. See Judges 4:4 (Deborah), 2 Kings 2:3 (sons of the prophets), 1 Kings 17 (Elijah), 1 Kings 18:13 (150 prophets). If God speaks through prophets in addition to those who wrote the Bible, how do we know whether they are true or false prophets? Jesus said that false prophets would be a sign that His coming is near. (Matthew 24:11, 24) In fact, the disciple John states, "Beloved, do not believe every spirit, but test the spirits, whether they are of God; because many false prophets have gone out into the world," 1 John 4:1.

◆ From your own background and understanding, discuss what you think would be tests to distinguish between a true and false prophet._____

The following are some of the biblical tests of a prophet. Discuss and list them.

Deuteronomy 13:1-4 _____
Isaiah 8:19, 20 _____
1 John 4:2, 3 _____
Matthew 7:15-20_____
Galatians 5:16-26 _____

◆ How should a modern-day prophet's message be considered?

___equal to the Bible writer
___inspired but not equal to a Bible writer
___a lesser light pointing to the Bible
___an authority above the Bible
___other_____

❏ How does God providing prophets to His people reveal His love for you?_____

The Seventh-day Adventist Church believes that the gift of prophecy was active in the ministry of Ellen White, one of the founders of the church. She ministered from 1844, when she was 17 years old, until her death in 1915.

Ellen White lived and worked in the United States, Europe, and Australia, counseling, preaching, writing, and assisting in establishing the work of the church. The organizational structure of the church, the medical ministry, the health message, and the educational system were guided by her. Ellen White never called herself a prophetess. She used the word *messenger,* because her work "covered so many lines."

As any other person, Ellen White must be tested by the biblical tests and be accountable to the authority of the Word of God.

❏ LIFEQUEST—Thoughtfully review these questions:
   ■ What does this topic tell me about God?
   ■ What difference does this topic make in my daily life?
   ■ How does this topic help me in my relationship with Jesus?

APPLICATION TO LIFE

Real Life

Steve thought he didn't have room for God in his schedule. But he had some questions about the Bible and the existence of God. Because of this, he decided to attend a seminar on Bible prophecy. During the seminar he was convinced of his need to learn more, and he began to attend church.

As Steve continued studying, he was at times caustic and critical about certain aspects of the Bible. He was especially judgmental when he studied the topic of spiritual gifts and discovered that the gift of prophecy was available today. He found it difficult to believe that God would speak in any manner to people today. When he discovered that some believe the gift of prophecy to have been given to Ellen White, a woman who lived in this century, he was truly skeptical.

Steve's pastor told him not to accept anyone's word concerning Ellen White or any other prophet, but to study for himself and make his own decision. Steve accepted the challenge and took a year and a half to carefully investigate. After doing so, Steve was convinced that God does use prophecy to share beneficial messages with modern-day Christians.

Your Turn

As you have studied this topic, it is exciting to discover that God is so concerned about His people that He has provided a means of communication with them. The gift of prophecy is an indication of how much God loves Christians. He wants His people to have every advantage possible, so He provides this important link.

If you have questions on this topic, continue studying and asking God to guide you in understanding. Remember to apply the scriptural tests of a prophet to determine whether the prophetic message and gift is from God.

Check the statements that most closely reflect your current feelings. (These are for personal reflection, not group discussion.)

___ I would like more study material about the gift of prophecy and Ellen White.

___ I accept the gift of prophecy as being an active gift in the Christian church.

___ I believe that the gift of prophecy was present in the life of Ellen White.

___ I would like to be baptized by immersion in the near future.

___ Other_____

Alone With God

Ask your group leader to give you a copy of the books *Steps to Christ* or *The Desire of Ages* by Ellen White. During your devotional time this week, read several pages of the book each day. This will assist you in becoming familiar with Ellen White and one of the books she wrote.

25

A Spirit-filled Life

GROUP LIFE

Growing Together—Group Closure

After this study guide, there is only one more in this series. As your group approaches the end of the series, there are probably various thoughts and questions in the minds of the members. There might even be some sadness. The group has enjoyed some special times together. The obvious question is, Now what do we do?

First, rejoice in the time of fellowship, friendship, and spiritual growth you have enjoyed together. Praise God for one another and in prayer, thank Him for the special times you have had together. Next, consider some possible options.

■ Your group might decide to keep on meeting without a break or to take a break of two or three weeks and then resume meeting again.

■ Not everyone's schedule will permit continuing to meet with the group. However, you can maintain the friendships you have formed.

■ If a member is not able to continue meeting with the group, the group leader could assist by providing Bible study materials for individual study.

As your group ends, make sure that no member feels that he is on his own without a support system of friends and prayer. Maintaining close relationships will assist each member of the group.

Sharing Life

As you consider your group, what have been the most significant experiences that have occurred in the group?

SCRIPTURE AND LIFE

WHAT JESUS SAID ABOUT THE HOLY SPIRIT

"But the Helper, the Holy Spirit, whom the Father will send in My name, He will teach you all things, and bring to your remembrance all things that I said to you."—John 14:26

As you study, be thinking about the LifeQuest questions:

■ What does this topic tell me about God?

■ What difference does this topic make in my daily life?

■ How does this topic help me in my relationship with Jesus?

If the average Christian were asked, "Where does the power received through prayer in the Christian life originate?" the answer would probably be, "With God." If the question were pressed further, the response would probably be, "God gives the Holy Spirit, who empowers us."

The subject of the Holy Spirit's ministry is vital to the Christian life.

❑ Select several of the following Scriptures to read, then discuss the questions. Write down evidence which helps you understand the Holy Spirit. John 16:13-15; Matthew 28:19; 1 Corinthians 12:7-11; Romans 15:30; Ephesians 4:30; Acts 5:3, 4.

◆ Is the Holy Spirit an influence—or a Person?_____

◆ What are some of the personal qualities of the Spirit?_____

_____

◆ What are the key points you discovered in the verses you just read?_____

_____

What is the job description assigned to the Holy Spirit? John

14:16, 17, 26; 15:26; 16:7-15; Acts 1:8.

_____

When and how do we receive the Holy Spirit? Acts 2:38, 39;
Ephesians 1:11-14; 1 John 4:12-16._____

_____

How often do you think one should pray for the Holy Spirit? Explain your answer. (Luke 11:9-13 says to ask . . .)

___ when someone accepts   ___when you feel the need of
    Jesus as Lord and Saviour.   God's presence in your
___daily   life.
___at baptism.   ___other _____

This scriptural summary reveals that the Holy Spirit is a member of
the Godhead and a Person with various emotions. The Spirit causes us
to want to accept Jesus as our Lord and Saviour. When we are converted
and the Holy Spirit dwells in us, His purpose is to make us like Jesus
and to empower us for ministry.

When we are filled with the Holy Spirit, we receive the fruits of the
Spirit in our lives—we become like Jesus in character and lifestyle.

In addition to helping us become like Jesus, the Spirit empowers us
for ministry. We are called to a life of prayer and service. The two cannot
be separated.

Three chapters in the Bible concentrate on the subject of spiritual
gifts. These are Ephesians 4, Romans 12, and 1 Corinthians 12. Ephesians
discusses the purpose of spiritual gifts, Romans the preparation necessary
to receive them, and 1 Corinthians how the gifts function in the church.

❑ Read 1 Corinthians 12. List the gifts mentioned. Briefly discuss
each and its application to the local church._____

_____

_____

◆ How many Christians receive gifts, and what determines
which gifts we receive?_____

◆ Discuss and apply the analogy of the human body and the church body to spiritual gifts and to our individual ministries.

_____

What do you believe are your spiritual gifts to be used in ministry? _____

(Note: If you have never filled out a questionnaire to assist you in understanding your gifts, ask your group leader for assistance. Your entire group may enjoy filling out a Spiritual Gifts questionnaire.)

❏ Read Romans 12:1-8. What is the "living sacrifice" God asks of each Christian?_____

List at least three items in your life that need to change for you to receive the power of the Holy Spirit. If you are comfortable with your lifestyle, then list at least three obstacles Satan attempts to throw across your path to keep you from being used by the Spirit.

_____

Write down what you plan to do to make Christian service a personal priority. _____

_____

❏ LIFEQUEST—Thoughtfully review these questions:
■ What does this topic tell me about God?
■ What difference does this topic make in my daily life?
■ How does this topic help me in my relationship with Jesus?

APPLICATION TO LIFE

Sheila's church had recently given her a job that involved leadership skills. When Sheila was asked to serve, she protested that she wasn't a leader. The congregation responded by saying, "We disagree—we believe you *do* have leadership skills." Sheila decided to accept the position, with the encouragement of her fellow Christians.

Several weeks later Sheila attended a workshop on "How to Share

Jesus." One of the seminars was on spiritual gifts. Sheila attended the seminar. One portion of the class involved filling out a questionnaire that would reveal the gifts God had given them. There was a time of silence as the class members filled out the material. The silence was broken as Sheila shouted, "I don't believe this! This test says that I have the gift of leadership!" Several in the class laughed at Sheila's outburst of surprise. Their response was, "Sheila, we tried to tell you, but you did not want to listen!"

Sheila—along with other members of the body of Christ—has been given Spirit-filled abilities to assist in the growth and development of the church on this earth. God has given a variety of gifts to make sure that no area of responsibility is overlooked. If Sheila had not used her God-given ability, the church would have suffered, and she would not have grown spiritually as God intended. Choosing not to use one's gift has a negative impact on the development of God's kingdom on this earth.

Your Turn

God has given you, as a Christian, a gift to use for Him. This gift (Spirit-filled ability) will do no one any good unless it is exercised. If you are not sure what God wants you to do for Him, or if you are hesitant about how to begin, ask your group for assistance.

Check the statements that most closely reflect your current feelings. (These are for personal reflection, not group discussion.)

___I would like to fill out a *Spiritual Gifts questionnaire* to discover my gifts.

___I know what my gifts are and desire assistance in using them.

___I accept Jesus as Lord and Saviour of my life and want to be baptized.

___I want to be ready to meet Jesus when He returns to this earth at His second coming.

___Other_____

Alone With God

During your prayer times this week, ask God to give you the desire to tell others about Him. Ask Him to provide you with opportunities to share Jesus.

26

Summarizing God's Message

GROUP LIFE

Growing Together—Daily Bible Study

Communication is vital to good relationships. Likewise, communication with God is vital to a growing relationship with Him. As your group comes to the end of its study, consider making a decision to do three things. First, decide to take time each day for Bible study. Second, make prayer a key ingredient of your day. Begin your day with prayer; end your day with prayer, and do not forget talking with God during the day. You can talk to Him while you are driving, working, at school, or involved in other activities. Third, make an agreement among your group members to meet together periodically for a time of sharing and fellowship.

Because your group may choose not to continue meeting to share and pray together, you may miss the support and fellowship of fellow Christians. There is spiritual strength in fellowship. Ask one of the group members to continue being your prayer partner. Periodically, the two of you can meet together to pray—or call each other on the phone. Never forget that God is your strength in all circumstances of life.

Sharing Life

Share with the group how they have assisted you in your personal and spiritual growth, or tell an experience from your participation in the group that was meaningful for you.

SCRIPTURE AND LIFE

Congratulations! You have now completed the study guides on the major themes of the Bible. As you have discovered, one can spend many hours on each individual topic. This study guide is a summary of the topics discussed in the LifeLine series, books one and two. The format will be somewhat different. Check those key points you feel you understand and discuss your questions. Following each summary, a life application question is given. Choose several to discuss, and have an excellent time!

❑ The Bible—both Old and New Testaments—is the written Word of God, given by divine inspiration through holy men who wrote, inspired by the Holy Spirit. The Bible reveals God's will and is the authority for doctrine and instruction for daily life. Daily Bible study and prayer is essential for all Christians.

◆ What is your favorite Bible text? Why is it special to you?

_____

❑ There is one God: Father, Son, and Holy Spirit; three separate eternal persons, yet one in character and purpose.

◆ If you had to tell someone what God means to you, what would you tell them?_____

❑ God is the Creator of all things. He created the world in six days and established the seventh day as a memorial to His creative work.

◆ What is your favorite item in all of God's creation?_____

_____

❑ We were made in the image of God with individuality and the power and freedom to think and act according to our choice. We are dependent upon God for daily life, salvation, and power to overcome sin.

◆ What does it mean to you to know that you are created in the image of God?_____

❑ All humanity is now involved in a great controversy between Jesus and Satan regarding the character of God, His law, and His sovereignty over the universe. Satan was once a created being in heaven, who rebelled and introduced sin to the universe.

◆ Share with your group one struggle in your life which you would like them to remember in prayer._____

❑ Jesus, a member of the Godhead, created all things. He also left heaven, came to this earth, died for the sins of mankind, and will return to this earth again.

◆ Share what it means to you to know that Jesus gave up all heaven for you. _____

❑ Christ's life of perfect obedience, and His suffering, death, and resurrection provides forgiveness and atonement for sin. Through faith, man can accept this free gift of God and receive salvation.

◆ If you have accepted Jesus as your personal Saviour, share with your group the circumstances surrounding your decision.

❑ By baptism, Christians express their faith in the plan of salvation and their love for God. They recognize that their sins are forgiven and express a desire to follow Jesus and His teachings. Baptism is by immersion—the same way Jesus was baptized.

◆ If you have been baptized, tell where you lived at the time and the details surrounding it.

❑ The church is a community of believers who confess Jesus as Lord and Saviour. The Bible says the church is like a body, with Christ as the head. In the last days, God's people (remnant) will keep the commandments of God and have the faith of Jesus.

◆ What does it mean to you to belong to God's family?

❑ The principles of God's law are embodied in the Ten Commandments. They express God's love, will, and purposes concerning human conduct and relationships and are a part of the Christian's life because of a love relationship with Jesus.

◆ Which commandment is your favorite? Why?

❑ Salvation is by grace alone—a free gift from God. The fruits of the Christian life reflect obedience to God's law because of a love relationship with Him.

◆ Why is it such a struggle for some Christians to obey Jesus?

❑ After the six days of creation, God rested on the seventh day and instituted the Sabbath as a memorial of Creation. God calls the Sabbath blessed and holy and states that no work is to be done on it. The Sabbath hours are from sunset to sunset, as stated in Genesis. The Sabbath is a perpetual sign of the special relationship between God and His people.

◆ What is your favorite activity to do on the Sabbath?

❑ The Sabbath (seventh day) was given to man at the end of the first week of creation. It was observed as God's holy day until a number of years after Christ's death. The day of worship was then changed by man from Saturday to Sunday.

◆ Why do you think the Sabbath is special to God?

❑ The hope of the world is the second coming of Jesus to this earth.

The Bible speaks of signs telling of Christ's coming. These signs appear in the physical, spiritual, social, moral, and political world.

◆ In your opinion, what sign of the end is most evident today?

_____

❑ Jesus' return will be literal, personal, visible, and worldwide. It will not be a secret coming, and everyone will see Him return.

◆ What do you think of when you hear the words "second coming?"

_____

❑ God, at the second coming, will give eternal life to those who accept Christ as Saviour and Lord. Until His coming, death is an unconscious state for all people. At Jesus' coming, the righteous dead are resurrected, and the living righteous are caught up into the air to be with Jesus. The second resurrection, of the unrighteous, will take place a thousand years later.

◆ Where would you like to be at the time of the resurrection?

_____

❑ The millennium is the thousand-year reign of Jesus in heaven between the first and second resurrections. Satan is bound to this earth while God's people are in heaven with Him. At the end of the millennium, the wicked are resurrected, and fire destroys them.

◆ What is your greatest fear concerning last-day events?

_____

❑ At the end of the millennium, after fire purifies the earth, God makes the earth new. The new earth will be the home of the redeemed. Sin, suffering, and death will be forever gone.

◆ Which result of sin will you be happiest to see destroyed?

_____

❑ There is a sanctuary in heaven, which the Lord set up. Christ ministers there on our behalf, making available to believers the benefits of His atoning sacrifice offered once for all on the cross. His intercessory ministry began at the time of His ascension. In 1844, at the end of the 2,300-day prophetic period, He entered the second and last phase of His atoning ministry. The sanctuary for Israel which Moses built was a pattern of the one in heaven.

◆ Why do you think God patterned the earthly sanctuary after the one in heaven?

❑ The 2300-day/year prophecy reveals the investigative judgment (cleansing of the sanctuary) which began in 1844. Also, the ministry, death, and resurrection of Jesus is predicted.

◆ Does the "judgment" make you afraid? Why—or why not?

❑ Christians are God's managers (stewards), entrusted by Him with time, abilities, possessions, and the earth and its resources. We are to faithfully serve Him and bring our tithes and offerings to Him.

◆ Tell how God has blessed you for being a faithful steward.

❑ Christians are called by God to be a people who think, feel, and act in harmony with the principles of heaven. Activities, including recreation, entertainment, and dress should reflect biblical principles. In addition, the principles of health, as outlined in the Scriptures, will be a part of the daily lifestyle.

◆ What is your favorite form of entertainment?

❑ God has created Christians with the need for fellowship, worship, Bible study/prayer, and interaction with others. In addition, God has given Christians the communion service and ordinance of humility (foot washing) to bind them together in unity and as a symbol of the plan of salvation.

◆ What to you is the most meaningful part of a worship service?

_____

❑ One of the gifts of the Holy Spirit is prophecy. This gift is an identifying mark of the last-day church (remnant). Seventh-day Adventists believe the gift was active in the ministry of Ellen White. All teachings and experience of a prophet must be tested by the Bible.
  ◆ Which prophet or prophetess in the Bible is your favorite? Why? _____

❑ God has given all members of His church spiritual gifts to use in ministry for the common good of the church and humanity. Given by the Holy Spirit, the gifts provide all abilities and ministries needed by the church to fulfill its function on earth.

◆ What is the spiritual gift you use most effectively for Jesus?

_____

APPLICATION TO LIFE

Real Life

One day a young man known as the "rich young ruler" approached Jesus and asked him, "Master, what must I do to have eternal life?" Jesus responded by telling him that the fruits of his devotion to God would be evident in following the commandments. The young man joyously responded by saying that he had kept the commandments since he was a young boy. Jesus then told him that he must be willing at any moment to sell everything that he owned and give it to the poor and to advance the kingdom of God. The Bible states that the young man became very sorrowful and walked away.

Many make the choice to wait until another day to make Jesus the number one priority in their lives. There are many modern-day "rich young rulers" walking the streets of your city or putting in time at their place of work simply to earn enough money to enjoy life and to buy a few pleasures. God is a distant reality to be dealt with later.

Your Turn

Many people wait for a personal tragedy to touch their lives before God is given serious consideration. Only when the fragility of life gives way to the results of sin does He become a high priority. But as you have studied these lessons on the teachings of Scripture, you have been given opportunities each week to make a decision for Jesus and begin to know the joy of a relationship with Him right now. When the teachings of these study guides are applied to your daily life by the power of the Holy Spirit, your life will be marked by a peace and happiness you have never experienced. This does not mean you will not have disappointments or tragedy in your life, but it does mean that you will have strength for today and hope for tomorrow.

Check the statements that most closely reflect your current feelings. (If you mark any of the responses listed below, please share them with your group leader.)

___I accept Jesus as Lord and Saviour of my life.
___I want to be baptized in the near future.
___I accept the Sabbath as being Saturday and desire to worship God on this special day.
___I want to become a member of the Seventh-day Adventist Church.
___I would like to spend more time with someone to discuss some unanswered questions.
___Other_____

Alone With God

Reflect upon your study and group experience as you have met over the past several weeks. What has been beneficial for your personal and spiritual growth? Thank God for the benefits you've received.